LINES·SEGMENTS·POLYGONS

LINES·SEGMENTS·POLYGONS

BY MINDEL & HARRY SITOMER

ILLUSTRATED BY ROBERT QUACKENBUSH

•

THOMAS Y. CROWELL COMPANY · NEW YORK

YOUNG MATH BOOKS

Edited by Dr. Max Beberman, Director of the Committee on
School Mathematics Projects, University of Illinois

Edited by Dorothy Bloomfield, Mathematics Specialist,
Bank Street College of Education

VENN DIAGRAMS *by Robert Froman*

Copyright © 1972 by Mindel and Harry Sitomer

Illustrations copyright © 1972 by Robert Quackenbush

L.C. Card 70-187941
ISBN 0-690-49485-8
0-690-49486-6 (LB)

1   2   3   4   5   6   7   8   9   10

LINES·SEGMENTS·POLYGONS

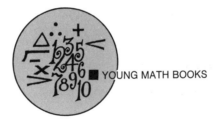

YOUNG MATH BOOKS

You know that a pencil drawn across a piece of paper makes a mark. That mark is a line. But that's not all there is to it.

Doodle or draw freely all over a piece of paper. Have you made different or funny shapes? All of them were made by lines.

If you look around you, you can see lines you never noticed before. The lines may be long or short, round, wavy, zigzag, or straight. This book is about STRAIGHT lines.

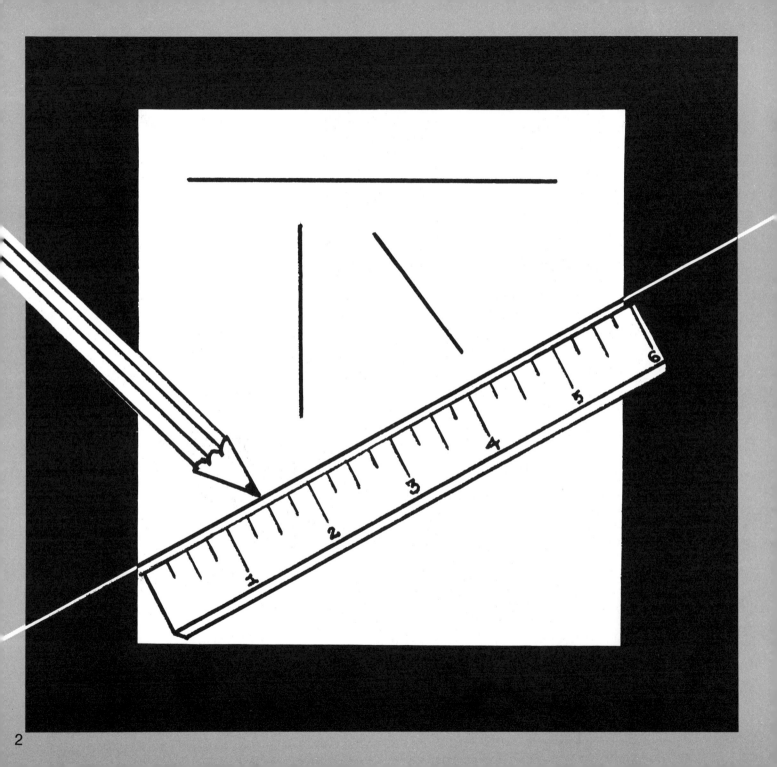

Try to draw a straight line on a piece of paper. It isn't easy to do. If you want your line to be really straight, you have to use a ruler or straightedge.

Straight lines can be horizontal, vertical, or slanting. If you had a ruler long enough, you could think about drawing a line going off your paper, out of the house, off the earth, and into space. You couldn't see it—but you can imagine it going on forever.

All straight lines go on and on without ending. When you see what you think is a line, you are really seeing only part of it. When you draw a line, you really draw only part of it. To show that a line goes on and on in both directions, let's put arrows at both ends, like this.

Lines are made up of POINTS. Even a small part of a line has so many of them they cannot be counted. All of them are exactly alike.

Sometimes some of the points on a line are important. Numbers are given to special points to help us measure things.

Suppose this bird feeder needs a new perch. The number **3** on the ruler tells that the old perch was three inches long. Now you know what size to make the new one.

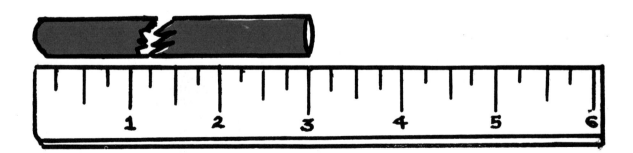

5

A •————————————————————————————→

Capital letters are sometimes used in naming points. For instance, take any point on a line and call it **A.** Now think of all the points on the line that are on the same side of **A.** This part of the line is a RAY. **A** names the endpoint of the ray.

A beam of light from a flashlight is like a ray.

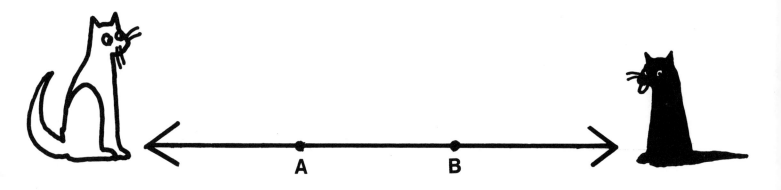

Or you can think about two points on a line and all the points between them. This part of a line is a SEGMENT. **A** and **B** name the endpoints of the segment. The segment itself is called **AB.**

The parts of lines you see in things are segments, because you can see where they start and where they end.

9

Rays and segments can be put together to make different shapes. When two rays are drawn from the same endpoint, they form an ANGLE. This endpoint is called the VERTEX of the angle. **A** names the vertex.

A

A

Angles can be large or small. The size of an angle depends only on how far apart the two rays are.

A special angle which looks like the square corner of this page is called a RIGHT ANGLE. This book has four of them on every page.

Angles are easy to find. Many roofs have them. So has your desk. Look around you. Can you find other angles?

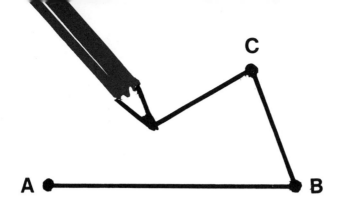

Here is something you can do with segments and angles. Put two dots on a piece of paper. Call them **A** and **B**. Now put a third dot anywhere on your paper. Be sure it is not on the same line with **A** and **B**. Call this dot **C**. Draw the segments that connect **A** to **B, B** to **C,** and **C** to **A.**

The shape you just made is a TRIANGLE. The segments **AB, BC,** and **CA** are the SIDES of the triangle. **A, B,** and **C** are its vertices. ("Vertices" means more than one vertex.) At each vertex, there is an angle.

Triangles can have different sizes and shapes, but every triangle has three sides and three angles.

Take three toothpicks and make a triangle. Each toothpick will be a side.

13

With more toothpicks you can make other figures. Put four of them together to form a figure with four sides. This is a QUADRILATERAL.

Quadrilaterals can have many shapes. Here are some of them.

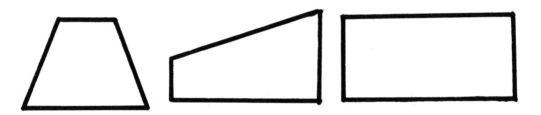

All triangles and quadrilaterals are POLYGONS. A polygon has three or more sides. It has the same number of angles as sides. The sides meet at their endpoints to make a CLOSED figure.

Not all figures are closed.  Is an angle closed?

15

When the sides of a polygon all have the same length, and its angles all have the same size, the polygon is called a REGULAR polygon. Can you tell what an IRREGULAR polygon is?

This is a regular triangle.

A regular quadrilateral is a SQUARE. Each of its angles is a right angle.

Regular triangles and squares are easy to make with toothpicks.

See how many kinds of irregular triangles and quadrilaterals you can make with your toothpicks. You can shorten some of the toothpicks to make different shapes.

Put five toothpicks together to make a PENTAGON. Have you seen a picture of the Pentagon Building in Washington?

17

A six-sided polygon is a HEXAGON. Bees build their honeycombs in shapes like these. Have you ever seen other hexagons?

Here is an easy way to make a regular hexagon with twelve toothpicks. Near the center of a piece of paper, put three toothpicks together to make a regular triangle. Make a dot at one vertex and call it **A.**

With the same vertex **A** and two more toothpicks, connect a second regular triangle to the first. Still with the same vertex **A,** add two more toothpicks for a third triangle.

Keep adding triangles to the ones you have already made. They will all have the same vertex **A.** You will end with six triangles. Do you see the regular hexagon?

Use toothpicks to make many-sided polygons. Can you ever make a circle with toothpicks?

Another way of making polygons is by using a geoboard. One kind of geoboard is a pegboard. You can use pegs and rubber bands to make polygons on it.

There is another kind of geoboard like a clock. You can make one for yourself. You will need a piece of wood about the size of this book, rubber bands or string, a pencil, and twelve toothpicks. You will also need twelve nails about two inches long and a hammer.

Place the toothpicks on your board to make a regular hexagon. Try to get the hexagon in the center of the board. Make a pencil dot on the board at each vertex of the hexagon. Take the toothpicks away. Your board will have six dots on it.

Imagine these dots are on a clock and write numbers for them. **12** will be at the top. Number the rest of the dots **2, 4, 6, 8, 10.**

The clockboard needs six more numbers. Guess where **1** should be. Put a dot there and number it. Do the same for **3, 5, 7, 9,** and **11.**

Hammer a nail partway in at each dot. Your clockboard is now ready. Each nail has its own number, and each can be used as a vertex of a polygon.

If you don't have a board, hammer, and nails, you can make a clockboard out of very thick cardboard, tacks, and string. The tacks will come out if you pull too hard on the string.

To make a regular triangle, loop a rubber band around **1, 5, 9.** If you use string, always be sure to go back to your first nail to close the figure.

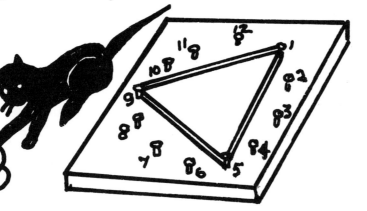

If you start at a different nail, and skip three nails each time, will you still get a regular triangle?

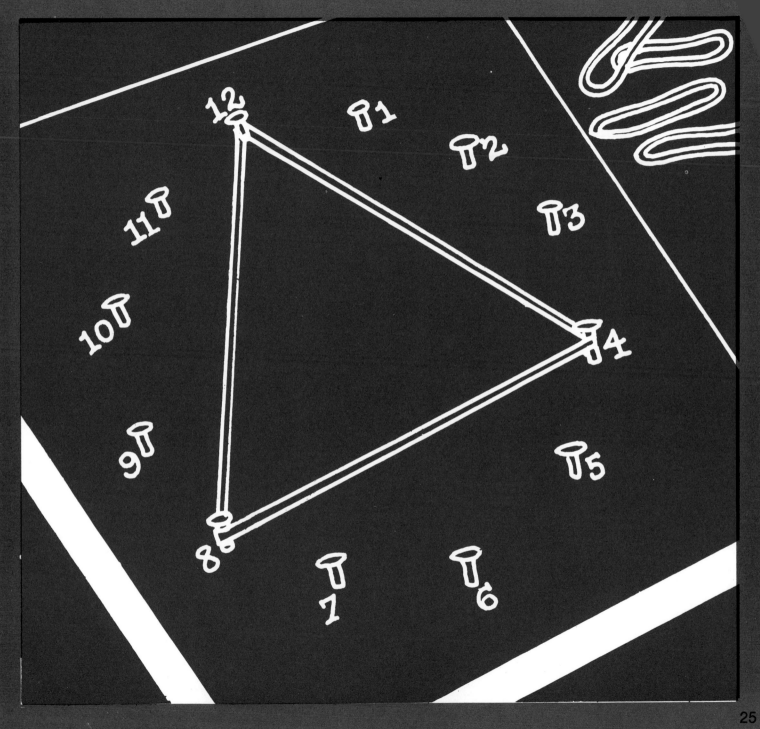

There are many kinds of irregular triangles you can make on your board. Try to find them for yourself. Here are two of them.

With your rubber band, loop around **12, 3, 9.** Can you fit a square corner into one of the angles of this triangle? Because it has a right angle in it, the triangle is called a RIGHT triangle.

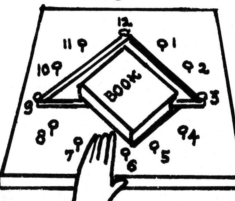

You can make another irregular triangle by looping a rubber band around **12, 5, 7.** In this triangle, two sides have the same length. This kind of triangle is called an ISOSCELES triangle.

Can you make other right and isosceles triangles? Do you have to start at **12**?

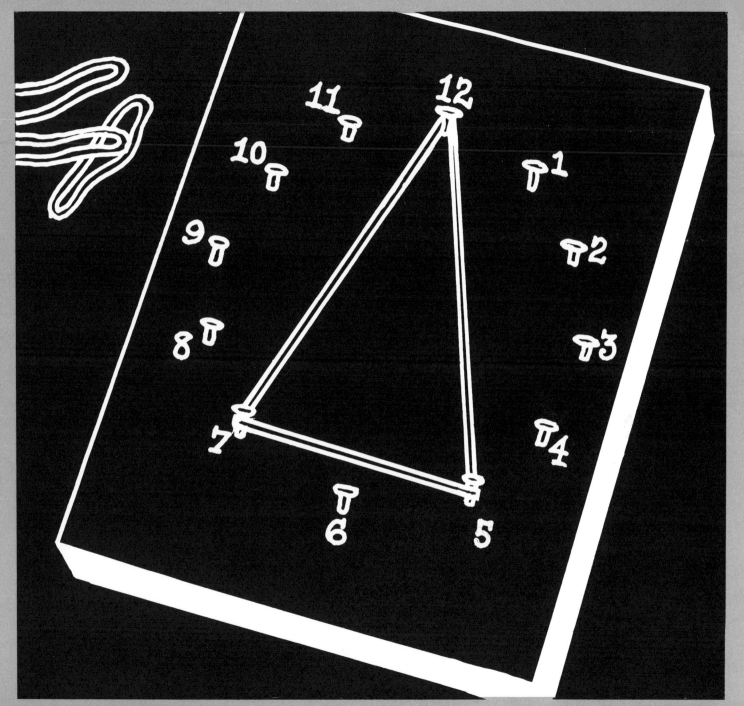

When you skip two nails each time with your rubber band, you make a square. Can you guess how to make irregular quadrilaterals? Here is one kind.

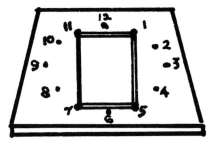

Loop around **1, 5, 7, 11.** This quadrilateral has four right angles like a square. Do the sides have the same length? This kind of quadrilateral is called a RECTANGLE.

Try to make irregular quadrilaterals that are not rectangles.

We started our clockboard with a regular hexagon. So you already know what happens when one nail is skipped each time. Now try to make irregular hexagons.

There is one more regular polygon you can make, using all your nails.

Here is an experiment. Make a square on your board. Connect one vertex of your square across the middle to the opposite vertex. Do the same with the other two vertices. How many triangles have you made in your square? Can you count more than four?

Try crossing from vertices to opposite vertices in different polygons and see what you come up with.

You can use your clockboard to make up games. Here is one. You have to copy this figure on your board with one piece of string. You may use only five of your nails. You may not go over the same side more than once, but you may go around any nail again. Here is a hint: Start at **10.** Go to **12,** to **2,** and then back to **10.** Can you finish it now?

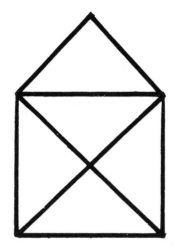

Can you do this one? Hint: Start at **9.**
Try to make up other games.

You can use differently colored rubber bands or strings to make interesting designs on your clockboard. Some artists use plywood or other hard surfaces, pretty fasteners, and threads of many colors to make beautiful decorations. Sometimes they use a board like your clockboard.

ABOUT THE ILLUSTRATOR

Robert Quackenbush was born in California and brought up in Arizona. He is a graduate of the Art Center College of Design in Los Angeles and also studied at Pratt Graphic Arts Center, Parsons School of Design, and the New School for Social Research in New York City.

Mr. Quackenbush has been a painter, teacher, and illustrator in New York City since 1956. He spends a great deal of time on painting excursions throughout Europe and the United States to replenish the exhibitions at the Robert Quackenbush Gallery of New York City and to paint and draw for his children's books. Mr. Quackenbush has illustrated fifty books for children and adults, for which he has received honors and citations from the Society of Illustrators and the American Institute of Graphic Arts. In addition, his art has been exhibited at leading museums throughout the country, including the Philadelphia Academy of Fine Arts and the Whitney Museum in New York City.

ABOUT THE AUTHORS

LINES, SEGMENTS, POLYGONS is the third book on which Mr. and Mrs. Sitomer have collaborated. Harry Sitomer, educated in New York City, has taught mathematics in high school and colleges, is the author of several mathematics textbooks, and has helped to compile many mathematics syllabi for the "new math." He is presently working as a coauthor on a textbook about linear algebra. He is also an enthusiastic cellist and gets much enjoyment from his regular sessions with amateur string quartets.

Mindel Sitomer, also educated in New York City as a biologist, found that their own two children and seven grandchildren had no difficulty in understanding large scientific concepts at an early age. Hence her enjoyment in working with her husband on these books for young readers. She is also an expert Braillist and is now transcribing into Braille a special assignment from the Library of Congress.

The Sitomers make their home in Huntington, New York.